How to Make the Best Cookies

Easy as 1-2-3

Happy Baking!

By

Michele Griesmer

Happy Darling!

Jaime Jansean

How to Make the Best Cookies Easy as 1 – 2 - 3

www.makethebestcookies.com
Copyright © 2018 Michele Griesmer

ISBN-13: 978-1717568281
ISBN-10: 1717568289

All rights reserved. No portion of this book may be reproduced mechanically, electronically, or by any other means, including photocopying, without permission of the publisher or author except in the case of brief quotations embodied in critical articles and reviews. It is illegal to copy this book, post it to a website, or distribute it by any other means without permission from the publisher or author.

Limits of Liability and Disclaimer of Warranty

The author and publisher shall not be liable for your misuse of the enclosed material. This book is strictly for informational and educational purposes only.

Warning – Disclaimer

The purpose of this book is to educate and entertain. The author and/or publisher do not guarantee that anyone following these techniques, suggestions, tips, ideas, or strategies will become successful. The author and/or publisher shall have neither liability nor responsibility to anyone with respect to any loss or damage caused, or alleged to be caused, directly or indirectly by the information contained in this book.

Publisher
10-10-10 Publishing
Markham, ON
Canada

Printed in Canada and the United States of America

Dedication

I dedicate this book to David, Christopher, Rachel, Sean, Judy, Alix, Jack, Trish, Mom and Dad.

Acknowledgements

This book would not have been possible without my wonderfully supportive family. My husband David, my taste tester, best friend and critic. My sons Sean and Christopher, who are both accomplished cooks.

Mom, a special thank-you. I'm sure you didn't realize what a true inspiration you have been, and will always be to me.

My daughter-in-law Judy, who has helped me with revisions, thank- you.

My best friend and mentor Trish Buzzone. Thanks friend for always being there.

So many recipes have been handed down to me. Many adapted from my favorite recipe publications, Bon Appetit, Saveur, the newspaper, those copied down in doctor's offices on scraps of paper, so a note of thanks to all my inspirations.

I have been so inspired to write my book, watching Vivian Howard on A Chefs Life, and reading her book Deep Run Roots.

Celia Rivenbark, author and columnist, has been such a delightful inspiration. I love her writing style and her sense of humor, thank you.

All my friends at Allen Park Rotary, especially Annette Preveaux.

All my friends at Southern Wayne County Regional Chamber, who gave me lots of opportunities to share my cookies. Leanna you are at the top of my list.

Grosse Ile Presbyterian Church, the cookie lady thanks you for allowing me to share my cookies with you. Carl and Carol Krohn made it special to be so appreciated.

A special thanks to Dashiell Parker, my photographer, for the wonderful job of making my cookies look as good as I know they taste.

The photographs would not have been nearly as good without the support and cooperation from The Seasoned Gourmet, a place for foodies, in Wilmington, North Carolina. Thank you so much for the use of your beautiful facility.

Thanks to all the wonderful behind the scenes people who helped me actually fulfill on a dream. A huge shout out, to all the folks at, Raymond Aaron Publishing. Jeannine for taking my beautiful pictures and designing my book cover, thank you. Mehran for patiently formatting my manuscript over and over again. My grammargal, Stacey thank you.

But, especially to my daughter Rachel, who from the time she was little asked, "Mama will you teach…"

About the Author

Michele Griesmer lives with her husband, David, and cat, Kitty. She divides her time between Topsail Island, North Carolina, and East Tawas, Michigan.

Michele's passion is cooking and baking and sharing that passion with others.

Content

Dedication ii

Acknowledgements iii

About the Author vi

Chapter 1 Tips and Tricks 1

Chapter 2 Drop Cookies 11

   a. Double Chocolate Chip Toasted Pecan Oatmeal Cookies 12

   b. Ginger Snaps 15

   c. Peanut Butter Cookies 17

   d. Chocolate Chip Cookies with Cream Cheese ... 19

   e. Cornmeal Cookies 21

   f. Lemon Crackled Sugar Cookies 23

   g. Chocolate and Walnut Cookies 25

Chapter 3 Bar Cookies 29

   a. Brownies 30

   b. Blonde Brownies – Congo Bars: Version 1 32

   c. Blonde Brownies – Congo Bars: Version 2 34

- d. Coffee Coconut Chews 36
- e. Sweet Chocolate Brownies with Cream Cheese 38
- f. Orange Chocolate Cheesecake Bars 41
- g. Lemon Bars..44
- h. Date Nut Squares 46

Chapter 4 Fruit Cookies..49
- a. Oatmeal Raisin..50
- b. Oatmeal Fruit Cookies 52
- c. Coconut Cream Jumbles 54
- d. Cape Cod Oatmeal Cookies.........................56
- e. Pistachio Cranberry Icebox Cookies.................59
- f. Rocks 61
- g. Brownie Cordial Cookies............................63

Chapter 5 Cut-Out Cookies...65
- a. Silver Bells...66
- b. Pepparkakor – Gingerbread 68
- c. Soft Sugar Cookie.......................................71
- d. The Santa Bear – Shape Cookie 74
- e. Crispy Sugar Cookie...................................76

f.	Cinnamon Stars 78

Chapter 6 Sandwich Cookies 81

g.	Rascals – Spitzbuben 82
h.	Peanut Butter Chocolate Chip 84
i.	Cocoa Peanut Butter Hearts 87
j.	Chocolate Sandwich Cookies with Coconut Filling 89
k.	Date Stacks 92

Chapter 7 Fancy or Ethnic Cookies 95

l.	Sonja Henies – Thumbprint 96
m.	Koulourakia 98
n.	Hard-Boiled Egg Gorabija 100
o.	Yugoslav Kifle 102
p.	Russian Tea Cakes 104
q.	Peanut Blossoms 106
r.	Chinese Almond Cookies 108

Chapter 8 Successes and Failures 111

a.	Beginners 112
b.	Making a Recipe the First Time 114
c.	Help for When You Are Experimenting 115

d. Ratio of Ingredients 117
e. Kids Love to Bake 118
f. Just Have Fun...119

Chapter 1

Tips and Tricks

Parchment vs. Buttering

Have you ever painstakingly rolled out beautifully shaped cookies, buttered your baking pan, gingerly laid out your cookies, and baked them; then waited patiently and attempted to lift them off your pan, only to see them crumble and crack right before your eyes? I have. For years this was my method. Shortening, butter, sprays, it really didn't matter…they always stuck.

Finally, I discovered parchment. It is a little more expensive, but magic when it comes to cookie removal. When you have catered and made hundreds of cookies like I have, parchment is well worth the added expense.

I even cheat. I'll use the same parchment repeatedly. However, I am very careful to use a fresh sheet if I'm baking a cookie with nuts, peanut butter, or chocolate, for example.

Give parchment a try. I'm certain you will be glad you did.

Why Use a Cookie Scoop?

Most cookie recipes call for either a teaspoon, a rounded teaspoon, or a tablespoon. These are all basically the same thing. It is not required for baking these recipes, but I'm all about making the best cookies, so I like using a cookie scoop for uniformity. There are many on the market, and they are basically just tiny ice cream scoops. The Vollrath Company, makes a Size 30 and a size 40. The 40 is smaller, approximately ¾ ounce; stainless steel bowl, plastic handle, and the one that I prefer. Some of my recipes yield over 100 cookies. With a scoop, that's 100 perfect 2 1/2- to 3-inch cookies, 12 to a standard cookie sheet. Do yourself a favor. It's a small investment for a perfectly uniform cookie, every time.

Let's say you don't want to make 100 cookies and all you need are 24. You can easily scoop out the remaining batter onto a cookie sheet and place the sheet in your freezer for at least an hour. Then label a plastic freezer bag, put the frozen cookie balls into the bag, and put the bag back in the freezer. The cookies are then ready the next time you have a hankering for fresh cookies.

So as not to think that a cookie scoop is one of those "uni-taskers" that will just sit in your kitchen drawer, it is also the perfect tool for meatballs.

Butter or Shortening?

I come from a long line of prolific bakers. My mother especially excelled. At Christmas she would give away cookie gifts to friends and neighbors. Her claim to fame was how many different kinds of cookies she would make and share. They were always beautiful and tasty.

One afternoon Mom and I went to visit a friend, and she put out a dish of cookies. I bit into a shape cookie, decorated with nuts and sugar, and went, "Wow, this is delicious! What recipe is this?" It was, you guessed it, one of my mother's signature cookie recipes. The difference was, it was made with butter, while my mother always used margarine. It was my aha moment, and I was eventually able to get my mother to convert to butter in her cookie baking as well. I was hooked.

I will, however, also share with you, the reader, recipes that call for margarine or shortening. Please don't read this as a typo. There are certain recipes that call for a combination of shortening or margarine and butter. It is all about texture. I could devote an entire chapter on the famous Nestle's Toll House Chocolate Chip Cookie. Some of my followers insist that they be made with Crisco, others only butter. It is a texture thing. I urge you to experiment. I will even share with you a recipe that uses lard. Again, it's a texture thing.

Crispy or Chewy?

I almost always prefer crispy, but I will share with you the simple secrets to making your cookies chewy. I'll use one of my signature cookies as an example, the Double Chocolate Chip, Toasted Pecan Oatmeal Cookie. After I place my cookies on a cookie sheet, I take another piece of parchment and lay it on top of all the cookies, then a second cookie sheet and press down to flatten the cookies. So it's like a cookie sandwich. Cookie sheet, parchment, cookies, parchment, cookie sheet. Flattening the cookies ensures I will get a crispy cookie. Leaving the cookies to flatten by themselves ensures a softer, chewier cookie. Sounds silly, but it's true.

Another way to get a softer cookie is to leave your finished product on the counter overnight. Your cookies will pull just enough humidity out of the air to keep them softer. Prefer crispy cookies? Place them in an airtight container.

Why Toast Nuts?

Yes, it's another step. Remember the title of the book is *Making the **Best** Cookies*. Whether the recipe calls for walnuts, pecans, or almonds, five minutes in the oven at 350 degrees makes a difference.

Your oven will be preheating anyway, so place your un-chopped nuts on your parchment-lined sheet, and bake. Cool, chop, and add to your favorite batter. The fragrance permeating your kitchen from toasting nuts will help you realize how this step will enhance your finished product. Trust me on this one: it's worth the extra step.

How to Adapt a Recipe?

The very first time I try a new recipe, I stick to the instructions and ingredients religiously. If I'm happy with the results, it usually becomes part of my repertoire to bake again.

I have already explained how I substitute butter for shortening, and of course that is your prerogative. Be careful here; there is a higher water-to-fat content in most shortenings on the market currently than in butter.

If the recipe calls for very expensive dark chocolate chips and what is in the cupboard is semi-sweet, substitute.

If the recipe calls for low-fat cream cheese or sour cream and what is in the fridge is full-fat, substituting it really won't make that much of a difference.

Of course, nuts are interchangeable; use what you have on hand.

Flours are not really good for substituting. I get asked about gluten-free; this is not my area of expertise. If you decide to use whole wheat rather than all-purpose flour, the results will be different.

If salt is a problem in your diet, it can easily be omitted.

Ask me a question. I will include my email address at the back of the book, and I would be delighted to assist you in adapting a recipe. Happy baking!

Chapter 2

Drop Cookies

Double Chocolate Chip Toasted Pecan Oatmeal Cookies

There are cookies and then there are cookies…this is one of my all-time favorites. What's not to love? Not one, but two kinds of chocolate chips, toasted pecans. They smell divine while baking and taste even better. Give them a try, they will become one of your favorites too.

- 5 cups oatmeal
- 4 cups flour
- 1 teaspoon salt
- 2 teaspoons baking powder
- 2 teaspoons baking soda
- 3 cups toasted pecans
- 2 cups milk chocolate chips
- 2 cups semi-sweet chocolate chips
- 2 cups unsalted butter
- 2 cups sugar
- 2 cups brown sugar
- 4 eggs
- 2 teaspoons vanilla extract

Preheat oven to 350 degrees. Line a standard cookie sheet with parchment paper. Toast pecans for 5 minutes, and then set aside to cool.

In a blender or food processor, blend oatmeal until it resembles cornmeal. Combine oatmeal with flour, salt, baking powder, and baking soda. Set aside.

In a food processor or by hand, chop pecans coarsely. Combine with chocolate chips and set aside.

Cream butter and sugars together in an electric mixer until fluffy. Add eggs one at a time, add vanilla, and mix well. Add dry ingredients. Stir in chocolate chips and chopped nuts.

Drop by cookie scoop or rounded teaspoon, 12 to a sheet. Bake 10 to 12 minutes, depending on your oven temperature, until golden. Allow to cool and rest for at least 2 minutes before removing to a cooling rack. This recipe yields about 106 cookies, and can easily be cut in half.

Ginger Snaps

Old fashioned ginger snaps. Hint…these are better than store bought.

- 2 cups flour
- 1/4 teaspoon salt
- 2 teaspoons baking soda
- 1 teaspoon cinnamon
- 1/4 teaspoon nutmeg
- 1 1/2 teaspoons ginger
- 1/2 teaspoon cloves
- 1/4 cup Crisco (white shortening)
- 1/2 cup unsalted butter
- 1 cup sugar
- 1 egg
- 1/4 cup honey
- zest of 1 lemon

Preheat oven to 375 degrees. Line a standard cookie sheet with parchment paper.

Combine flour with salt, baking soda, and spices; stir and set aside.

In an electric mixer, cream Crisco and butter. Add sugar and beat until creamy. Add egg, honey, and lemon zest. Add dry ingredients.

Drop by cookie scoop or rounded teaspoon, 12 to a sheet. Bake 10 to 12 minutes, depending on your oven, until golden. The cookies will puff and flatten and look crinkly as they cool. Allow to cool at least 2 minutes before removing to a cooling rack. This recipe yields about 30 cookies.

Peanut Butter Cookies

One bite of these peanut butter cookies will have you nabbing them off the cookie sheet before they're cool, they are that good. Crunchy and chewy all at the same time, this recipe is the real deal. Double the recipe, they go fast.

- 2 1/2 cups flour
- 1 1/2 teaspoons baking soda
- 1/2 teaspoon salt
- 1 cup unsalted butter
- 1 cup sugar
- 1 cup brown sugar
- 1 1/2 cups peanut butter
- 2 eggs

Preheat oven to 350 degrees. Line a standard cookie sheet with parchment paper.

Combine flour, baking soda, and salt. Set aside.

In an electric mixer, cream butter and sugars until light and fluffy. Add peanut butter and eggs one at a time. Add dry ingredients gradually, until combined.

Drop by cookie scoop or rounded teaspoon, 12 to a sheet. Dust fork in flour and make cross marks on each cookie. Bake 10 to 12 minutes, depending on your oven, until golden. Let rest on the cookie sheet at least 2 minutes before removing to a cooling rack. This recipe yields about 48 cookies.

Chocolate Chip Cookies with Cream Cheese

This is a delicious twist on a favorite. Something magical happens when cream cheese, lemon extract, coconut and chocolate chips come together. I have been making these for so many years; I don't even remember where the recipe came from. Try these once and they will become a family favorite.

- 2 cups flour
- 3/4 teaspoon salt
- 1/2 teaspoon baking powder
- 1 cup unsalted butter
- 3 ounces of cream cheese
- 1 1/4 cup sugar
- 2 eggs
- 1 teaspoon vanilla extract
- 1/4 teaspoon lemon extract
- 1 cup semi-sweet chocolate chips
- 1/2 cup coconut

Preheat oven to 350 degrees. Line a standard cookie sheet with parchment paper.

Combine flour, salt, and baking powder in a bowl and set aside.

In an electric mixer, cream butter and cream cheese. Add sugar and beat until light and fluffy. Add eggs one at a time, then vanilla and lemon extract. Add dry ingredients. Stir in chocolate chips and coconut.

Drop by cookie scoop or rounded teaspoon, 12 to a sheet. Bake until lightly brown on the edges, about 15 minutes, depending on your oven. Let rest on the cookie sheet at least 2 minutes before removing to a cooling rack. This recipe yields about 40 cookies.

Cornmeal Cookies

I know it sounds weird, cornmeal in a cookie. Don't knock it until you have tried them. The cookies turn out chewy, crunchy and melt in your mouth all at the same time.

- 1 1/2 cups flour
- 1/2 cup cornmeal
- 1/2 teaspoon salt
- 3/4 cups unsalted butter
- 3/4 cups sugar
- 1 egg
- 1 teaspoon vanilla extract

Preheat oven to 350 degrees. Line a standard cookie sheet with parchment paper.

Combine flour, cornmeal, and salt in a bowl. Sset aside.

In an electric mixer, beat butter until light and fluffy. Add sugar. Add egg and vanilla and mix well. Gradually add dry ingredients.

Drop by cookie scoop or rounded teaspoon, 12 to a sheet. Bake 14 to 16 minutes, depending on your oven, until golden. Let rest on the cookie sheet at least 2 minutes before removing to a cooling rack. This recipe yields about 26 cookies.

Lemon Crackled Sugar Cookies

This is a family favorite. Make a cup of tea, and sit down and enjoy a soft, cakey, delicious lemon cookie. I make the big size for my grand-children and whenever we are together they are always a request.

- 5 cups flour
- 2 teaspoons baking soda
- 2 teaspoons cream of tartar
- 1 cup unsalted butter
- 1 cup margarine
- 3 cups sugar
- 6 eggs
- 3 teaspoons orange extract
- 3 teaspoons lemon extract
- zest of 1 lemon
- 1/2 cup sugar for sanding

Preheat oven to 350 degrees. Line a standard cookie sheet with parchment paper.

Combine flour, baking soda, and cream of tartar. Set aside.

In an electric mixer, cream butter, margarine, and sugar until light and fluffy. Add eggs one at a time. Add flavorings and zest. Stir in dry ingredients and mix well. The batter will be soft.

Take a cookie scoop or rounded teaspoon of batter and gently roll it in the reserved sugar. Place 12 on a cookie sheet. Bake about 12 minutes, depending on your oven, until golden. Allow cookies to rest at least 2 minutes before removing to a cooling rack. They come out of the oven puffy but shrink and get crackly. This recipe yields about 60 cookies. This cookie also lends itself well to making large 4-inch cookies. To do so use 2 cookie scoops or rounded teaspoons instead of 1 for each cookie. Only 6 of these larger cookies will fit on a sheet.

Chocolate and Walnut Cookies

Very crunchy, on the outside, soft and gooey on the inside. If that sounds good to you, they are amazing.

- 2 cups flour
- 1 tablespoon kosher salt
- 1 1/4 teaspoon baking soda
- 1 cup toasted walnuts
- 2 cups semi-sweet chocolate chips
- 1 cup unsalted butter
- 1 1/4 sugar
- 1 1/2 cups brown sugar
- 2 eggs
- 1 tablespoon vanilla extract

Preheat oven to 325 degrees. Line a standard cookie sheet with parchment paper. Toast walnuts for 5 minutes; set aside to cool.

In a small bowl, combine flour, salt, and baking soda. Set aside.

In a food processor, combine cooled nuts and chocolate chips. Process until finely chopped, and set aside.

Using an electric mixer, cream butter and sugars together until fluffy. Add eggs, one at a time, beating well after each addition. Add vanilla. Gradually add the dry ingredients and nut and chocolate mixture.

Drop by cookie scoop or rounded teaspoon, 12 to a sheet. Flatten slightly. Bake about 15 minutes, depending on your oven, until golden. Allow cookies to rest at least 2 minutes before removing to a cooling rack. They come out of the oven puffy but deflate. This recipe yields about 60 cookies.

Chapter 3

Bar Cookies

Brownies

Not all brownies are created equal. This is a consistently delicious brownie recipe. I suggest making a double recipe, once they are cool enough to cut, they will be gone.

- 2/3 cups flour
- 1/2 teaspoon baking powder
- 1/3 cup cocoa powder
- 7 tablespoons butter or margarine
- 1 cup sugar
- 2 eggs
- 1 teaspoon vanilla extract
- 1/2 cup walnuts (optional)

Preheat oven to 350 degrees. Grease an 8- or 9-inch square baking pan.

In a bowl combine flour, baking powder, and cocoa powder. Set aside.

In an electric mixer, cream butter and sugar. Add eggs one at a time, mixing well after each addition. Add vanilla. Gradually add dry ingredients. The batter will be stiff. Stir in nuts and pour into prepared baking pan.

Bake 25 minutes, depending on your oven. A toothpick inserted in the middle should come out clean. Cool in pan. Cut into squares. This recipe yields 9 to 12 brownies and can easily be doubled using a 9x13 baking pan.

Blonde Brownies – Congo Bars: Version 1

Both versions make a fast and easy desert. If there is not enough time to make a tray of cookies, this is a delicious time saver. Another easy recipe to double, just a suggestion, everyone will be happy that you did.

- 2 2/3 cups flour
- 2 1/2 teaspoons baking powder
- 1/2 teaspoon salt
- 2/3 cups unsalted butter
- 2 1/4 cups brown sugar
- 3 eggs
- 1 cup chopped walnuts
- 1 cup semi-sweet chocolate bits

Preheat oven to 350 degrees. Grease an 8- or 9-inch square baking pan.

In a bowl combine flour, baking powder, and salt. Set aside.

In an electric mixer, cream butter and brown sugar. Add eggs one at a time, mixing well after each addition. Gradually add dry ingredients; the batter will be stiff. Stir in nuts and chocolate chips. Pour into prepared baking pan.

Bake 25 minutes, depending on your oven. A toothpick inserted in the center should come out clean. Cool in pan and cut into squares. This recipe yields 9 to 12 brownies. It can easily be doubled in a 9x13 baking pan.

Blonde Brownies – Congo Bars: Version 2

- 2 cups flour
- 1 teaspoon baking powder
- 1/4 teaspoon salt
- 2/3 cups unsalted butter
- 2 cups brown sugar
- 2 eggs
- 2 teaspoons vanilla extract
- 1 cup chopped walnuts
- 1 cup semi-sweet chocolate bits

Preheat oven to 350 degrees. Grease an 8- or 9-inch square baking pan.

In a bowl combine flour, baking powder, and salt. Set aside.

In an electric mixer, cream butter and brown sugar. Add eggs one at a time, mixing well after each addition. Add vanilla. Gradually add dry ingredients; the batter will be stiff. Stir in nuts and chocolate chips. Pour into prepared baking pan.

Bake 25 minutes, depending on your oven. A toothpick inserted in the middle should come out clean. Cool in pan and cut into squares. This recipe yields 9 to 12 brownies and can easily be doubled in a 9x13 baking pan. This is the chewier recipe, though both are good.

Coffee Coconut Chews

This is a different bar cookie. The coffee and the cinnamon are a lovely combination, and a tasty complement to the sweetness of the coconut.

Bottom layer:

- 2 cups flour
- 2 teaspoons cinnamon
- 1 tablespoon instant coffee
- 1 cup unsalted butter
- 1 cup sugar
- 2 egg yolks

Top layer:

- 2 egg whites
- 1/4 cup sugar
- 1 cup coconut

Preheat oven to 350 degrees. Grease a 9x13-inch baking pan.

Bottom layer:

In a bowl combine flour, cinnamon, and instant coffee. Set aside.

In an electric mixer, cream butter and sugar. Add egg yolks one at a time, mixing well after each addition. Gradually add dry ingredients; the batter will be crumbly. Press into prepared baking pan.

Top layer:

Beat egg whites until foamy. Add sugar and stir in coconut, and spread over batter.

Bake 25 minutes, depending on your oven, until golden. A toothpick inserted in the middle should come out clean. Cool in pan, and cut into squares. This recipe yields 24 bars.

Sweet Chocolate Brownies with Cream Cheese

These are rich and delicious. A tiny bit more work, but worth the extra effort. Wait until your first bite, they are bound to become a family favorite. They are elegant enough for company, and a hit when asked to bring a desert.

Chocolate batter:

- 4-ounce German sweet chocolate bar
- 3 tablespoons unsalted butter
- 2 eggs
- 3/4 cup sugar
- 1/2 teaspoon baking powder
- 1/4 teaspoon salt
- 1/2 cup flour
- 1/2 cup chopped walnuts
- 1 teaspoon vanilla extract
- 1/4 teaspoon almond extract

Cream cheese mixture:

- 2 tablespoons unsalted butter
- 3 ounces cream cheese
- 1/4 cup sugar
- 1 tablespoon flour
- 1/2 teaspoon vanilla extract

Preheat oven to 350 degrees. Grease an 8- or 9-inch square baking pan.

Chocolate batter:

In a small microwave-safe bowl, melt chocolate with 3 tablespoons of butter; cool and set aside.

Beat 2 eggs until light in color. Add sugar, baking powder, salt, and flour. Blend in chocolate mixture and nuts, vanilla, and almond extract. Set aside.

Cream Cheese Mixture:

In an electric mixer, cream butter with cream cheese. Gradually add sugar. Add egg, flour, and vanilla. Set aside.

Spread about half of chocolate batter in the bottom of greased baking pan. Spread the cream cheese mixture over the top. Spoon on remaining chocolate batter and run a knife through both batters to swirl and marbleize. Bake 35 to 40 minutes depending on your oven. A toothpick inserted in the middle should come out clean. Cool in pan; cut into squares. This recipe yields 16 to 20 squares.

Orange Chocolate Cheesecake Bars

I like to call these bars, baby cheese cakes in a chocolate crust. Everything works, the chocolate, the toasted nuts, the sour cream, cream cheese with that lovely orange zest.

Crust:

- 1 cup flour
- 3 tablespoons cocoa powder
- 1 teaspoon baking powder
- 1/2 cup sugar
- 1/4 teaspoon salt
- 1/2 cup unsalted butter
- 1 egg yolk - reserve white for filling
- 1 teaspoon vanilla extract
- 1/2 cup chopped pecans

Filling:

- 8 ounces cream cheese
- 1/3 cup sugar
- 1/2 cup sour cream
- 1 tablespoon flour
- grated zest of 1 orange
- 1/4 teaspoon salt
- 1 whole egg
- 1 egg white
- 1/2 teaspoon vanilla or orange extract

Preheat oven to 325 degrees. Grease and flour an 8- or 9-inch square baking pan.

Crust:

In a food processor or large bowl, combine flour, cocoa powder, baking powder, sugar, and salt. Through the feeding tube or in the bowl beat in butter, 1 tablespoon at a time. Add yolk, vanilla, and pecans. Press into the bottom of a prepared pan. Bake 15 minutes.

Filling:

In a food processor or small bowl, beat cream cheese, sugar, sour cream, flour, orange zest, and salt until smooth. Beat egg, reserved white, and vanilla or orange extract.

Pour the filling over the warm crust. Bake 20 to 25 minutes. A toothpick inserted in the middle should come out clean. Remove and let cool at least 1 hour. It's best if refrigerated overnight. This recipe yields 16 bars.

Lemon Bars

Rich, sweet, lemony and delicious; these bars are destined to become a family favorite, as they are mine.

Crust:

- 1/2 cup unsalted butter
- 1 cup flour
- 1/4 cup confectioner's sugar

Filling:

- 2 eggs
- 1 cup sugar
- 2 tablespoons lemon juice
- 2 tablespoons flour
- 1/2 teaspoon baking powder
- grated zest of 1 lemon

Preheat oven to 350 degrees. Grease an 8- or 9-inch square baking pan.

Crust:

In a food processor or small bowl, combine butter, flour, and confectioner's sugar. Press into a prepared baking pan. Bake 15 minutes, and set aside to cool. Crust should be golden.

Filling:

Mix together eggs, sugar, lemon juice, remaining flour, baking powder, and lemon zest.

Pour filling into cooled crust and bake 25 minutes. Let cool in pan before cutting. This recipe yields 9 to 12 bars.

A WORD OF CAUTION! THIS RECIPE DOES NOT LEND ITSELF TO DOUBLING IN A 9X13 PAN. USE TWO 8- OR 9-INCH SQUARE PANS. TRUST ME HERE.

Date Nut Squares

Chewy, sweet and delicious, sure to be a crowd pleaser.

- 3 cups dates, chopped
- 1 cup brown sugar
- 1 cup water
- 1/2 cup chopped walnuts
- 3/4 cups unsalted butter
- 1/2 cup sugar
- 1 1/4 cups flour
- 1 1/4 cup oatmeal
- 1 teaspoon salt

Preheat oven to 350 degrees. Grease a 9x13-inch cake pan.

Combine dates, brown sugar, and water in a saucepan. Bring to a boil, and then cool until thickened, about 5 minutes. Add walnuts and stir. Set aside.

In an electric mixer, cream butter and sugar. Add flour, oatmeal, and salt; mixture will be crumbly. Press two-thirds of the oatmeal mixture into the bottom of prepared baking pan. Spread the date mixture on top, then cover with remaining oatmeal mixture. Pat lightly. Bake 30 minutes, until golden. This recipe yields 24 squares.

Chapter 4

Fruit Cookies

Oatmeal Raisin

A familiar favorite, oatmeal raisin with nuts; what sets it apart are three things. Toasting the nuts, cinnamon and blending the oatmeal, together they make a delicious chewy cookie, an old stand-by but better.

- 3 cups toasted walnuts
- 5 cups oatmeal
- 4 cups flour
- 1 teaspoon salt
- 2 teaspoons baking powder
- 2 teaspoons baking soda
- 2 teaspoons cinnamon
- 4 cups raisins
- 2 cups butter
- 2 cups sugar
- 2 cups brown sugar
- 4 eggs
- 2 teaspoons vanilla extract

Preheat oven to 350 degrees. Toast walnuts for 5 minutes. Set aside to cool.

In a blender or food processor, blend oatmeal until it resembles cornmeal. Combine oatmeal with flour, salt, baking powder, baking soda, and cinnamon. Set aside.

In food processor or by hand chop nuts, coarsely. Combine with raisins and set aside.

Cream butter and sugars together in an electric mixer until fluffy. Add eggs one at a time; mix well. Add vanilla. Add dry ingredients. Stir in raisins and chopped nuts.

Not crowding, place 12 scoops or rounded teaspoons on a standard cookie sheet. For a crispy cookie, flatten the dough. (See Chapter 1.) Bake 10 to 12 minutes, depending on your oven temperature, until golden. Allow cookies to cool and rest for at least 2 minutes before removing to a cooling rack. This recipe makes approximately 106 cookies, and can easily be cut in half.

Oatmeal Fruit Cookies

All these yummy things in one cookie; are a sure winner. The end result is a chewy delicious cookie with all the fruit flavors working together.

- 4 cups oatmeal
- 1 cup flour
- 1 teaspoon cinnamon
- 1 teaspoon baking soda
- 1 cup butter
- 1 cup sugar
- 1 cup brown sugar
- 2 eggs
- 1 teaspoon vanilla extract
- 1 cup coconut
- 1 cup chopped dates
- 1 cup walnuts
- 1 cup raisins

Preheat oven to 350 degrees. Line a standard cookie sheet with parchment.

In a food processor, blend oatmeal until it resembles cornmeal. Combine with flour, cinnamon, and baking soda. Set aside.

In an electric mixer, cream butter and both sugars. Add eggs one at a time, blending well after each addition. Add vanilla. Gradually add dry ingredients.

Stir in fruit and nuts. Do not crowd. Place 12 scoops or rounded teaspoons, on a standard cookie sheet. Bake 10 to 12 minutes, depending on your oven temperature, until golden. Allow cookies to cool and rest for at least 2 minutes before removing to a cooling rack. This recipe yields approximately 48 cookies.

Coconut Cream Jumbles

Take a tray of these to your next function and watch people's faces. They are such a surprise. To quote one of my favorite chefs, it's a party in your mouth.

- 2 cups cake flour
- 1/2 teaspoon salt
- 1/2 teaspoon baking powder
- 3/4 cup butter
- 1 cup sugar
- 2 egg yolks
- 1 teaspoon orange zest
- 1 teaspoon lemon zest
- 1 tablespoon lemon juice
- 1 cup coconut
- 3/4 cup sour cream

Preheat oven to 375 degrees. Line a standard cookie sheet with parchment.

Sift cake flour, salt, and baking powder. Set aside.

In an electric mixer, cream butter and sugar until light and fluffy.

Add egg yolks, one at a time, blending well after each addition. Add both zests and lemon juice. Add sifted dry ingredients. Stir in coconut and sour cream.

Drop by cookie scoop or rounded teaspoon onto the prepared cookie sheet, 12 cookies to a sheet. Bake 10 to 12 minutes, depending on your oven, until golden around the edges. Allow cookies to cool and rest for at least 2 minutes before removing to a cooling rack. This recipe yields approximately 48 cookies.

Cape Cod Oatmeal Cookies

I began the book by telling you that, yes lard does show up in cookies. Trust me here, it does make a difference. These are so good you will start keeping dates and lard on hand.

Cookie:

- 1 cup butter, or 1/2 cup butter and 1/2 cup lard
- 1 3/4 cups flour
- 1 teaspoon baking soda
- 1 teaspoon cinnamon
- 1 cup sugar
- 2 eggs
- 1 tablespoon molasses
- 1/2 cup chopped dates or raisins
- 1/2 teaspoon salt
- 1 3/4 cups oatmeal
- 1/2 cup chopped walnuts

Filling:

- 8 ounces chopped dates
- 3/4 cup water
- 3/4 cup sugar
- 1 teaspoon vanilla extract

Preheat oven to 375 degrees. Line a standard cookie sheet with parchment.

Cookie:

Melt 1 cup of butter, or 1/2 cup of butter and 1/2 cup of lard, in the microwave and set aside.

Combine flour, baking soda, and cinnamon in a small bowl and set aside.

In an electric mixer, combine melted butter or lard with sugar and beat well. Add eggs, one at a time, beating well after each addition. Add molasses and continue beating. Gradually add dry ingredients. Stir in dates or raisins. Set aside and prepare filling.

Filling:

In a saucepan combine dates with water, sugar, and vanilla.

Bring to a boil, reduce heat, and simmer 5 minutes.

Drop cookie mixture by cookie scoop or rounded teaspoon onto the prepared cookie sheet, 12 cookies to a sheet. Place teaspoonful of filling on top and cover with another cookie scoop or rounded teaspoon of batter. Gently flatten.

Bake 12 to 15 minutes, depending on your oven, until golden. Allow cookies to cool and rest for at least 2 minutes before removing to a cooling rack. This recipe yields approximately 12 cookies.

Pistachio Cranberry Icebox Cookies

Make these and keep a roll in your freezer, after the first time you make them you will see why. A tiny cookie, that packs a real flavor punch.

- 1 1/2 cups flour
- 1/4 teaspoon salt
- 1/2 teaspoon cinnamon
- 3/4 cup unsalted butter
- 1/3 cup sugar
- 1/2 cup chopped pistachios
- 1/3 cup chopped dried cranberries
- 1/2 orange zest
- 1 egg, beaten
- 1/4 cup sanding sugar

Preheat oven to 350 degrees. Line a standard cookie sheet with parchment.

In a small bowl, combine flour, salt, and cinnamon, and set aside.

In an electric mixer, cream butter and sugar until light and fluffy. Add dry ingredients, pistachios, cranberries, and orange zest.

Remove from mixer and shape into an 8 1/2-inch long tube, about 1 1/2 inches wide. Brush with beaten egg and roll in sanding sugar. Wrap dough tube in plastic wrap or wax paper and chill for at least 2 hours.

Remove from plastic wrap and cut into 1/4-inch slices. Place 12 cookies on a cookie sheet and bake for 10 to 12 minutes. Allow cookies to cool and rest for at least 2 minutes before removing to a cooling rack. This recipe yields approximately 24 cookies.

Rocks

If any cookie name is a misnomer it would be this one. They are soft and chewy, even though, the nuts and dates, in the light colored cookie batter, do look a little like a rock, they are not.

- 2 cups boiling water
- 2 cups chopped dates
- 2 teaspoons baking soda
- 2 cups unsalted butter
- 4 cups brown sugar
- 6 eggs
- 7 cups flour
- 2 cups walnuts

Preheat oven to 375 degrees. Line a standard cookie sheet with parchment.

Pour boiling water over dates and baking soda and let cool.

In an electric mixer, cream butter and sugar. Add eggs one at a time, blending well after each addition.

Gradually add flour. Add date mixture. Mix well. Add walnuts.

Drop by cookie scoop or rounded teaspoon onto the parchment-lined cookie sheet, 12 cookies to a sheet. Bake 10 to 12 minutes, depending on your oven, until golden around the edge. Allow cookies to cool and rest for at least 2 minutes before removing to a cooling rack. This recipe can easily be cut in half, and yields at least 72 cookies.

Brownie Cordial Cookies

Cordial refers to cherries, and with coconut and chocolate, oh my. These cookies are soft and chewy and so flavorful.

- 3 cups flour
- 3/4 cup cocoa powder
- 1 1/2 teaspoons baking powder
- 1/8 teaspoon salt
- 2/3 cup unsalted butter
- 4 tablespoons vegetable oil
- 2 cups sugar
- 4 eggs
- 1 cup maraschino cherries
- 2 tablespoons cherry liquid
- 1 cup coconut

Preheat oven to 350 degrees. Line a standard cookie sheet with parchment paper.

In a small bowl, combine flour, cocoa powder, baking powder, and salt. Set aside.

In an electric mixer, cream butter, vegetable oil, and sugar until light and fluffy, add eggs one at a time, blending well after each addition. Gradually add dry ingredients. Stir in cherries, cherry liquid, and coconut.

Drop by cookie scoop or rounded teaspoon onto the parchment-lined cookie sheet, 12 cookies to a sheet. Flatten slightly with a floured glass or use my method for crispy cookies in Chapter 1. Bake 18 minutes, depending on your oven, until lightly browned. Allow cookies to cool and rest for at least 2 minutes before removing to a cooling rack. This recipe yields approximately 66 cookies.

Chapter 5

Cut-Out Cookies

Silver Bells

Silver bells are crispy on the outside with a slightly soft interior. A perfect holiday cut out cookie, frosted, dusted with sprinkles or sanding sugar, they are delicious.

Cookie:

- 2 1/4 cups flour
- 1/4 teaspoon salt
- 1 cup unsalted butter
- 1/2 cup confectioner's sugar
- 1 teaspoon vanilla extract

Frosting:

- 1 cup confectioner's sugar
- 1/2 teaspoon vanilla extract
- 1 to 1 1/2 tablespoons water

Preheat oven to 375 degrees. Line a standard cookie sheet with parchment.

Cookie:

In a small bowl, combine flour and salt. Set aside.

In an electric mixer, cream butter and sugar. Add vanilla and gradually add dry ingredients. Mix until it just comes together.

Roll on a lightly floured surface to 1/4-inch thick. Cut into desired shapes. Place 12 to a prepared cookie sheet. Bake 10 to 15 minutes, depending on your oven, until lightly browned on the edges. Let cookies cool at least 2 minutes on the cookie sheet before removing to a cooling rack.

Frost when completely cool. Alternately, sprinkle with colored sanding sugars, before baking.

Frosting:

In a small bowl, combine confectioner's sugar, vanilla, and water to the desired consistency. (This frosting tends to be runny). Add food coloring if you wish.

Once frosted, the cookies should sit for at least an hour before storing. This recipe yields 30 cookies.

Pepparkakor – Gingerbread

Pronounced: pepper-a-ka-kor. This is a soft gingerbread cookie recipe, sure to please. There is nothing like the smell of gingerbread cookies in the oven.

Cookies:

- 5 cups flour
- 1 1/2 teaspoons baking soda
- 2 to 3 teaspoons ginger
- 1 teaspoon cinnamon
- 1 teaspoon ground cloves
- 1 cup unsalted butter
- 1 cup sugar
- 1 egg
- 1 cup molasses
- 2 tablespoons white vinegar

Royal Icing:

- 1-pound confectioner's sugar
- 3 egg whites
- 1/2 teaspoon cream of tartar
- 1 teaspoon lemon juice

Preheat oven to 375 degrees. Line a standard cookie sheet with parchment.

Cookies:

In a small bowl, combine flour, baking soda, ginger, cinnamon, and cloves. Set aside.

In an electric mixer, cream butter and sugar. Add egg and beat to combine. Add molasses and vinegar. Mixture may curdle; this is normal. Gradually add dry ingredients. Mix until it just comes together.

Roll on lightly floured surface, 1/8 inch thick. Cut into desired shapes. Place 12 to a prepared cookie sheet. Bake 6 minutes, depending on your oven, until lightly browned. Let cookies cool at least 2 minutes on the cookie sheet before removing to a cooling rack. This recipe easily yields one hundred 3-inch shape cookies.

Frost, when completely cool. Alternately, sprinkle with colored sanding sugars before baking. Once frosted, the cookies should sit for at least an hour before storing.

Royal icing:

Combine all ingredients in a metal bowl. Keep covered with plastic wrap until ready to use.

Soft Sugar Cookie

I know, twelve and quarter cups, of cake flour is a tremendous amount. Bear in mind it is easy to cut this recipe in half, the batter freezes beautifully. The cookies are soft and melt in your mouth delicious. The frosting just makes them party cookies.

Cookies:

- 12 1/4 cups cake flour
- 4 tablespoons baking powder
- 2 tablespoons salt, divided
- 1 1/2 pounds butter
- 3 2/3 cups sugar
- 4 eggs
- 3/4 cups milk
- 1 1/2 tablespoons vanilla

Soft Party Cookie Frosting:

- 4 cups confectioner's sugar
- 1/2 cup Crisco (white shortening)
- 5 tablespoons milk
- 1 teaspoon vanilla extract
- food coloring (optional)

Preheat oven to 325 degrees. Line a standard cookie sheet with parchment.

Cookies:

Sift together cake flour, baking powder, and 1 tablespoon of salt.

In the largest bowl of your electric mixer, cream butter, sugar, and other tablespoon of salt until light and fluffy. Add eggs one at a time, and beat well after each addition. Slowly add milk and vanilla. Beat well.

Gradually add dry ingredients. Mix until it just comes together. Chill in plastic wrap for at least 1 hour.

Roll on lightly floured surface to 1/4 an inch thick. Cut into desired shapes. Place 12 to a parchment-lined baking sheet. Bake 10 to 15 minutes, depending on your oven, until lightly browned. Let cookies cool at least 2 minutes on the cookie sheet before removing to a cooling rack.

Frost, when completely cool. Alternately, sprinkle with colored sanding sugars before baking. Once frosted, the cookies should sit for at least 1 hour before storing.

This is a huge recipe. It can easily be cut in half. It stores well in the freezer. This recipe easily yields over one hundred 3- to 4-inch shape cookies.

Soft Party Cookie Frosting:

In a large bowl, beat sugar and Crisco. Add milk and vanilla. Add food coloring if desired.

The Santa Bear – Shape Cookie

It is hard to say, which is my personal favorite, sugar cookie, that is why I have included four different varieties. The Santa Bear is crunchy, that combination of Crisco (white shortening) and butter that gives this cookie its unique texture.

Cookies:

- 3 1/2 cups flour
- 1/2 teaspoon baking powder
- 3/4 cup unsalted butter
- 2/3 cups Crisco (white shortening)
- 3/4 cup sugar
- 1 egg
- 1/4 teaspoon vanilla extract

Frosting:

- 6 cups confectioner's sugar
- 1 teaspoon vanilla extract
- 9 to 10 tablespoons milk
- food coloring (optional)

Preheat oven to 350 degrees. Line a standard cookie sheet with parchment.

In a small bowl, combine flour and baking powder.

In an electric mixer, cream butter, Crisco, and sugar until light and fluffy. Add egg and vanilla, and beat well.

Gradually add dry ingredients. Mix until it pulls away from the side of the bowl.

Roll on lightly floured surface to 1/4 of an inch thick. Cut into desired shapes. Place 12 to a parchment-lined baking sheet. Bake 10 minutes, depending on your oven, until very lightly browned. Let cookies cool at least 2 minutes on the cookie sheet before removing to a cooling rack.

Frost, when, completely cool. Alternately, sprinkle with colored sanding sugars before baking. Once frosted, the cookies should sit for at least 1 hour before storing.

Frosting:

Combine all ingredients. Add food coloring if desired.

Crispy Sugar Cookie

Just like the name implies, a crispy sugar cookie. Different than Santa Bear, a very nice and delicious cut out cookie just the same.

- 3 cups flour
- 3/4 teaspoon baking powder
- 1/4 teaspoon salt
- 1 cup unsalted butter
- 1 cup sugar
- 1 egg
- 1 tablespoon milk
- 1 teaspoon vanilla extract

Preheat oven to 375 degrees. Line a standard cookie sheet with parchment.

In a small bowl, combine flour, baking powder, and salt. Set aside.

In bowl, of electric mixer, cream butter and sugar until light and fluffy. Add egg, milk, and vanilla, and beat well.

Gradually add dry ingredients. Mix until batter comes together.

Remove from bowl and cover with plastic wrap. Refrigerate for at least 2 hours.

Roll on lightly floured surface to 1/4 of an inch thick. Cut into desired shapes. Place 12 to a prepared cookie sheet. Bake 10 minutes, depending on your oven until lightly browned. Let cookies cool at least 2 minutes on the cookie sheet before removing to a cooling rack. This recipe easily yields thirty-six 3-inch shape cookies.

Frost, when completely cool. Alternately, sprinkle with colored sanding sugars before baking. Can be frosted with any of the previous frosting recipes.

Cinnamon Stars

Cinnamon stars are a beautiful cinnamon color and delicious. Do make them in a star shape. They are so pretty and so tasty.

Cookies:

- 2 cups flour
- 2 1/2 teaspoons cinnamon
- 1/2 teaspoon salt
- 1 cup walnuts
- 1 cup sugar
- 1/2 cup unsalted butter
- 2 eggs

Icing:

- 2 egg whites or 2 teaspoons powdered egg white and 2 tablespoons water
- 1 1/4 cups confectioner's sugar
- 1/2 cup finely chopped walnuts

Preheat oven to 325 degrees. Line a standard cookie sheet with parchment.

Cookies:

In a small bowl, mix flour, cinnamon, and salt. Set aside.

In a food processor, pulse walnuts with 2 tablespoons of sugar until finely ground. Do not grind into a paste.

In an electric mixer, cream butter and remaining sugar until light and fluffy. Add eggs one at a time, blending well after each addition. Add nut mixture, and gradually add dry ingredients until just blended.

Roll on lightly floured surface to 1/4 of an inch thick. Cut into star shapes. Place 12 to a prepared cookie sheet. Bake 10 minutes, depending on your oven, until lightly browned. Let cookies cool at least 2 minutes on the cookie sheet before removing to a cooling rack. This recipe easily yields seventy-two 3-inch shape cookies.

Icing:

Whisk together egg whites and sugar. Spread a thin layer of icing on cooled cookie. Sprinkle with walnuts.

Chapter 6

Sandwich Cookies

Rascals – Spitzbuben

I always make these with a tiny cookie cutter, they are a melt in your mouth treat. Pronounced: Spits-bu-ben. Delicious and festive.

- 1 teaspoon vanilla extract
- 1/2 cup sugar
- 1 cup unsalted butter
- 2 cups flour
- 1/2 teaspoon lemon zest
- 1 egg, separated
- 1 extra egg yolk
- 2/3 cup strawberry jam

Preheat oven to 325 degrees. Line a standard cookie sheet with parchment.

Mix vanilla extract and sugar together and set aside.

Combine butter, flour, vanilla and sugar mixture, lemon zest, and 2 egg yolks to make a dough. Roll it out on a lightly floured surface until it is about 1/4 of an inch thick. Use a cookie cutter to cut into stars or desired shape, making sure to have an even number.

Place 12 cookies to a prepared cookie sheet, and brush lightly with beaten egg white. Bake for 20 minutes, or until lightly browned. Allow to rest at least 2 minutes on the cookie sheet before removing to a wire rack to cool completely.

Spread half the cookies with jam. Arrange the other half on top, to make cookie sandwiches. Brush tops with egg white and sprinkle with granulated sugar. This recipe yields between 20 and 24 cookies.

Peanut Butter Chocolate Chip

Oh my gosh, these are so good. Have you ascertained yet that I am a cookie freak. The cookies themselves are melt-in-your mouth goodness. Compound that with a chocolate peanut butter filling, these are amazing.

Cookies:

- 1 3/4 cups flour
- 1 teaspoon baking powder
- 1 teaspoon baking soda
- 1/2 teaspoon salt
- 6 tablespoons unsalted butter
- 1/2 cup peanut butter
- 9 tablespoons brown sugar
- 14 tablespoons confectioner's sugar
- 1 egg
- 1/2 cup vegetable oil
- 1/2 teaspoons vanilla extract
- 1 1/3 cups chocolate chips

Filling:

- 3 ounces chocolate chips
- 1/4 cup peanut butter
- 2 tablespoons confectioner's sugar
- 1/4 teaspoon salt
- 6 tablespoons half and half or evaporated milk

Preheat oven to 350 degrees. Line a standard cookie sheet with parchment.

Cookie:

Combine flour, baking powder, baking soda, and salt. Set aside.

In an electric mixer, cream butter, peanut butter, brown and confectioner's sugar until light and fluffy. Add egg, oil, and vanilla. Gradually add reserved dry ingredients. Add chocolate chips.

Dropping by cookie scoop or rounded teaspoon, 12 to a prepared cookie sheet. Bake 10 to 12 minutes, depending on your oven until lightly browned. Allow to rest at least 2 minutes before moving to a cooling rack. Make sure you have an even number.

Filling:

In microwave melt chocolate chips. Beat in peanut butter, confectioner's sugar, salt, and half and half or evaporated milk.

When cookies are cool, spread a small amount of the filling on one cookie and cover with second cookie. This recipe yields approximately 24 cookies.

Cocoa Peanut Butter Hearts

It wouldn't be Valentine's Day if these lovely sandwich cookies didn't appear on my table. It's another one of those to take to a gathering and watch people's faces, the chocolate, the subtle peanut butter and the raspberry…got to say it again. It's a party in your mouth. They are like a chocolate peanut butter shortbread, leave them out over-night and they get soft, so good.

- 2 cups flour
- 1/2 cup cocoa powder
- 1/2 teaspoon baking powder
- 1 cup unsalted butter
- 1 cup sugar
- 1/2 cup confectioner's sugar
- 2 teaspoons vanilla extract
- 1 egg
- 1 cup peanut butter
- 2 cups milk chocolate chips
- strawberry jelly

Preheat oven to 375 degrees. Line a standard cookie sheet with parchment.

In a separate bowl mix flour, cocoa powder, and baking powder. Set aside.

In an electric mixer, cream butter, sugar, confectioner's sugar, and vanilla until light and fluffy. Add egg and peanut butter, beat well. Gradually add dry ingredients. Chill dough in the refrigerator at least 1 hour.

Roll dough out on a lightly floured surface until it is about 1/8 of an inch thick. Use a cookie cutter to cut into hearts. Use a smaller heart cookie cutter, or a smaller circle cutter, to cut out the center of half the cookies, making sure to have an even number of each.

Place 12 of the cookies to a prepared cookie sheet. Bake cookies approximately 8 minutes, depending on your oven, until lightly browned. Allow to rest at least 2 minutes before moving to a cooling rack. While cookies are baking melt chocolate chips in microwave.

When cookies are cool, spread a small amount of the melted chocolate on the solid heart and place a small amount of jelly on top of the chocolate frosted heart. Then cover with the second cookie with the cut out heart. These are delicate, so do not press hard. This recipe yields approximately 24 cookies.

Chocolate Sandwich Cookies with Coconut Filling

Chocolate cookies with German Sweet Chocolate Frosting filling, what's not to like.

Cookies:

- 1 3/4 cups flour
- 3/4 cup cocoa powder
- 3/4 teaspoon baking powder
- 1/4 teaspoon salt
- 3/4 cup butter
- 1 1/2 cups sugar
- 2 eggs
- 2 tablespoons milk
- 1 teaspoon vanilla extract
- 1/2 cup chopped pecans

Coconut Pecan Filling:

- 1/2 cup butter
- 1/2 cup brown sugar
- 1/4 cup light corn syrup
- 1 cup chopped pecans
- 1 cup toasted sweetened coconut
- 1 teaspoon vanilla extract

Preheat oven to 350 degrees. Line a standard cookie sheet with parchment.

Cookies:

In a separate bowl, mix flour, cocoa powder, baking soda, and salt. Set aside.

In an electric mixer, cream butter, sugar and confectioner's sugar until light and fluffy. Add eggs, milk, and vanilla, and beat well. Gradually add reserved dry ingredients. Stir in pecans.

Dropping by a standard cookie scoop or rounded teaspoon, place 12 to a prepared cookie sheet. Bake 10 to 12 minutes, depending on your oven, until golden. Allow to rest at least 2 minutes before moving to a cooling rack. Make sure you have an even number. Put

2 cookies together with a small amount of Coconut Pecan Filling in between.

Coconut Pecan Filling:

In a small saucepan, melt butter, sugar and corn syrup. Stir on medium heat until bubbly and thick. Add nuts, coconut, and vanilla.

Date Stacks

Keep trying my date cookie recipes and you will keep dates in your baking cupboard. These are chewy and sweet and absolutely delicious.

Cookies:

- 3/4 cups butter
- 1 1/2 cups flour
- 1 1/2 cups oatmeal
- 2 teaspoons baking powder
- 1 teaspoon baking soda
- 1 cup brown sugar
- 4 tablespoons milk

Date Filling:

- 1 cup sugar
- 1/2 teaspoon vanilla extract
- 1 cup chopped dates
- 1 cup water

Preheat oven to 375 degrees. Line a standard cookie sheet with parchment.

Cookies:

In an electric mixer or food processor, combine all ingredients; like a pie crust.

Roll out dough on a lightly floured surface to a 1/8-inch thickness. Cut into shapes. Make sure you have an even number of cookies. Place 12 to a prepared cookie sheet. Add a scant teaspoon of date filling on top of each cookie, and top with another cookie. Bake 10 to 12 minutes, depending on your oven, until lightly browned. Allow to rest at least 2 minutes before moving to a cooling rack.

Date Filling:

In a small saucepan, combine all ingredients and cook on medium heat until thickened.

Chapter 7

Fancy or Ethnic Cookies

Sonja Henies – Thumbprint

Yes, Sonja Henie was an Olympic ice skater in the 1930's. And yes she was a movie star about the same time. Why did they name a cookie after her? Who can say. What I do know is these are delicious. It just wouldn't be the holidays at my house without them. There are thumb print cookies out there, but these the jam or jelly is added after baking. Makes a difference. Try them.

- 1/2 cup butter
- 1/4 cup brown sugar
- 1 egg yolk
- 1 cup flour
- reserved egg white
- 1/2 cup ground walnuts
- 1/2 cup coconut
- jelly or jam

Preheat oven to 350 degrees. Line a standard cookie sheet with parchment.

In an electric mixer, cream butter and sugar. Add egg yolk and gradually add flour.

Scoop out cookie balls. Roll dough in your hands to make a round ball. Roll cookie ball first in egg white, then either ground walnuts or coconut. Place 12 cookies to a prepared cookie sheet. Before baking, make a depression with your thumb in the center of each cookie. Bake approximately 15 minutes, depending on your oven, until golden. Allow to rest at least 2 minutes before removing to a cooling rack to cool completely.

Fill with your favorite jam or jelly.

Note: This is a very small recipe. Doubling the recipe will yield about 27 cookies.

Koulourakia

Pronounced: Koo-Lou-rack-e-yah. Greek figure eight cookies. They are lightly sweet and cakey. Different and make a beautiful presentation on a cookie platter.

- 1 cup butter
- 1/2 cup sugar
- 2 eggs (save one yolk for glaze)
- 1 tablespoon orange juice
- 1 teaspoon baking powder
- 1 teaspoon vanilla extract or whiskey
- 3 cups flour
- sesame seeds

Preheat oven to 350 degrees. Line a standard cookie sheet with parchment.

In an electric mixer, cream butter and sugar. Add egg, orange juice, baking powder, and vanilla or whiskey, and gradually add flour.

With a cookie scoop, scoop out a portion of dough; roll dough in your hands to make a ball. Take the round ball and shape it into a tube, about 3 inches long. Put the two ends together, then twist, making a figure eight. Repeat until all cookies are formed.

Place the reserved egg yolk on a flat dish with a teaspoon of water, and mix. Dip each figure eight into the egg mixture, then into the sesame seeds. Place 15 cookies to a prepared cookie sheet and bake approximately 15 minutes, depending on your oven, until cookies are golden. Allow to rest at least 2 minutes before removing to a cooling rack to cool completely. This recipe yields approximately 30 cookies.

Hard-Boiled Egg Gorabija

Pronounced: Go-ra-bee-ya. These are cookies I grew up with, I believe they are Serbian. It sounds like a lot of eggs, they are delicious. Rich, festive and guests will ask for the recipe.

- 1-pound butter
- 1 cup sugar
- 2 eggs
- 10 hard-boiled egg yolks (sieved)
- 4 cups flour
- 1/2 cup sugar
- 1 cup ground walnuts

Preheat oven to 350 degrees. Line a standard cookie sheet with parchment.

In an electric mixer, cream butter and sugar; add eggs and sieved egg yolks. Gradually add flour. Mix well. Form dough into a large ball and roll out on a lightly floured surface to 1/4 of an inch thick. Cut into desired shapes.

Combine sugar and ground nuts, sprinkle small amount on each cookie.

Place 12 cookies to a prepared cookie sheet and bake approximately 15 minutes, depending on your oven, until cookies are golden. Allow to rest at least 2 minutes before removing to a cooling rack to cool completely. This recipe yields approximately 48 cookies.

Yugoslav Kifle

I know, it's a little bit of work, but oh is it worth the effort. The cookies melt in your mouth, and they're so pretty. Try them and you will be hmm, hmming too.

Cookies:

- 2 cups flour
- 1 tablespoon dry yeast
- 1/2 cup butter
- 1/2 cup sour cream
- 2 egg yolks
- Confectioner's sugar

Walnut Filling:

- 3 cups ground walnuts
- 1 cup sugar
- 1 cup water
- 1 teaspoon cinnamon

Cookies:

In an electric mixer fit with a bread hook, or in a large food processor, place flour and yeast. Pulse or mix until combined. Add butter, sour cream, and egg yolks. Mix well. Knead until mixture comes together. Divide into three parts; chill at least 1 hour.

Now preheat oven to 375 degrees. Line a standard cookies sheet with parchment.

Dust your work surface lightly with confectioner's sugar. Roll into a circle and cut into pie wedges. Fill each wedge with a small amount of the walnut filling, or apricot jam. Roll from the wide end to the narrow end, forming a crescent. Place 12 to a prepared cookie sheet. Bake approximately 25 minutes, depending on your oven, until cookies are puffed and golden. Allow to rest at least 2 minutes before removing to a cooling rack to cool completely. Dust with confectioner's sugar. This recipe yields approximately 36 cookies.

Walnut filling:

In a small bowl combine walnuts, sugar, water and cinnamon.

Russian Tea Cakes

No it is not a misprint. These lovelies bake at 250 degrees for an hour. The kitchen will smell so good; the family will be standing at the oven waiting.

- 1/2-pound butter
- 5 tablespoons sugar
- 1 teaspoon vanilla extract
- 1 cup finely ground pecans
- 2 cups flour
- confectioner's sugar for dusting

Preheat oven to 250 degrees. Line a standard cookie sheet with parchment.

In an electric mixer, cream butter, sugar, and vanilla. Add pecans and gradually add flour.

Scoop or spoon out cookie balls. Roll dough in your hands to make a round ball. Note: if using a standard cookie scoop, before rolling into a ball, I cut these in half. They are a very delightfully rich cookie. One-bite size is enough.

Place 24 cookies to a prepared cookie sheet and bake approximately 1 hour. Allow to rest briefly, and then roll in confectioner's sugar while still warm. When completely cool, roll again in confectioner's sugar. This recipe yields approximately sixty 1/2-scoop cookies.

Peanut Blossoms

Another holiday must have at our house. They are soft and once that Hershey's Kiss goes in to the cookie, they are gooey and delicious.

- 1 3/4 cups flour
- 1 teaspoon baking soda
- 1/2 cup butter
- 1/2 cup peanut butter
- 1/2 cup sugar
- 1/2 cup brown sugar
- 2 tablespoons milk
- 1 egg
- 1 teaspoon vanilla extract
- additional sugar for dusting
- 30 Hershey's Kisses

Preheat oven to 375 degrees. Line a standard cookie sheet with parchment.

In a separate bowl, combine flour and baking soda.

In an electric mixer, cream butter, peanut butter, and sugars; add milk, egg, and vanilla. Gradually add dry ingredients.

Scoop out cookie balls. Roll dough in your hands to make a round ball. Roll cookie balls in additional sugar.

Place 12 cookie balls to a prepared cookie sheet. Bake 10 to 12 minutes, depending on your oven, until lightly browned. While still warm, press a Hershey's Kiss into each cookie. The cookies must be completely cool and chocolate hardened before stacking. This recipe yields 30 cookies

Chinese Almond Cookies

Yep, just like the ones in the Chinese restaurant. A little crunchy and soft on the inside and so good.

- 3 cups flour
- 1 1/2 teaspoons baking soda
- 1 cup Crisco (white shortening) or lard
- 1/4 cup light corn syrup or honey
- 1 cup sugar
- 1 egg
- 3 tablespoons almond extract
- 1 cup blanched whole almonds
- optional yellow food coloring

Preheat oven to 375 degrees. Line a standard cookie sheet with parchment.

In a separate bowl, combine flour and baking soda.

In an electric mixer, cream Crisco or lard, corn syrup or honey, and sugar; add egg and almond extract. Add food coloring if desired. Gradually add dry ingredients.

Scoop out cookie balls. Roll dough in your hands to make a round ball. Gently flatten each cookie, and place an almond in the center of each. Place 12 cookie balls to a prepared cookie sheet. Bake approximately 20 minutes, depending on your oven, until golden. Allow to rest at least 2 minutes before removing to a cooling rack to cool completely.

This recipe yields approximately 48 cookies.

Chapter 8

Successes and Failures

Beginners

Everyone starts out a beginner, so here are a few words of advice:

The basic ingredients for your cookie kitchen include the following:

- All-purpose flour
- Confectioner's sugar
- Baking powder
- Baking soda
- Kosher salt
- Oatmeal
- Walnuts
- Pecans
- Coconut
- Raisins
- Cinnamon
- Cloves
- Ginger
- Eggs
- Granulated sugar
- Brown sugar

- Pure vanilla extract
- Pure lemon extract
- Pure almond extract
- Unsalted butter
- Crisco (white shortening)
- Margarine
- Molasses
- Light corn syrup
- Sprinkles

Equipment:

1. A stand mixer. This is not essential, but it does make the job easier. A hand mixer will do.
2. A food processor. This is also not essential, but it, too, makes the job easier.
3. Wooden spoons.
4. Spatulas, silicon or rubber.
5. A fish turner. It sounds weird, but it is the best thing I have found for removing cookies from the tray.
6. Assorted mixing bowls.
7. Measuring spoons and cups.
8. 1-cup and 1-quart liquid measuring cups.

Making a Recipe the First Time

Read the recipe from the beginning to the end; it will ultimately save you some time.

The first time I make a recipe, I inventory my supplies to make sure I have everything. If not, it's off to the store. Or a different recipe.

Make the recipe exactly as the recipe calls for. Don't substitute. As you become more experienced, there are certain things you can change. But do yourself an enormous favor: follow the recipe exactly as written the first time through.

Measure out your ingredients in separate bowls. That one little extra step will help to guarantee your cookie success every time. If you take the time to put all your dry ingredients in a separate bowl—the eggs, the sugar, even chocolate chips, nuts, or coconut—all your ingredients are there in front of you, so the likelihood of forgetting something is significantly reduced.

Help for When You Are Experimenting

Once you have had some experience with different types of cookie baking, then allow yourself to experiment.

No raisins? Try dried cranberries or cherries.

No nuts, or allergic? Skip them, and try adding more chocolate chips or fruit.

Butter instead of margarine or shortening? By all means, experiment. A Toll House Chocolate Chip Cookie will have a uniquely different texture just by your choice of fats.

Cut-out sugar cookies are a very interesting example of how different ratios of ingredients affect the way a cookie will taste.

If there is a greater amount of wet ingredients, you will get a chewier cookie.

If you use confectioner's sugar instead of granulated, your cookie will be lighter, almost flaky.

If you use brown sugar over granulated sugar, the cookie will be chewier.

The different proportions will yield a different cookie.

Different flours: whole wheat works, but it tends to produce a tougher cookie.

Ratio of Ingredients

As you familiarize yourself with recipes, you will begin to see certain patterns:

A specific amount of butter to a specific amount of sugar. Usually it is 1 part fat to 2 parts sugar.

A certain amount of wet ingredients to dry.

An average large egg measures 1/4 cup. Keep that in mind if you are short on eggs and have a reserved white or yolk on hand.

Kids Love to Bake

Don't keep cookie baking to just the adults.

Kids truly love to bake.

Even when they are small, give them a piece of dough and a small rolling pin and let them play.

Let them sit on the counter, with you, and hand you measured-out ingredients.

Sprinkles, how they love sprinkles and frosting.

As they grow, bring up a chair and let them help, measure, and add.

I was a Girl Scout leader for many years and worked full time. I had as many as sixteen girls at any given time, so I did not always have the time to plan out a craft for the girls on meeting night. When I announced that tonight we were going to bake cookies, they were delighted. I am sad to report only half of the girls present had ever made cookies before.

Let them help you mess up the kitchen. It will leave a lasting impression.

Just Have Fun

The most important thing about cookies is having fun. Don't stress.

I've thrown out batters…oops, forgot the sugar, or these are terrible.

Make it fun.

Nothing smells as wonderful as cookies in the oven.

Cookies are a feel-good food.
Talk about how to make friends or family smile: bring out a plate of freshly baked cookies.